Ages Eterna

Purest Affections, Navigating In Glowing Rhythms, and Heartfelt Yearnings

Subodh Das

BookLeaf Publishing
India | USA | UK

Made with ❤ on the BookLeaf Publishing Platform
www.bookleafpub.in
www.bookleafpub.com

Dedicated to YOU

Whose name is woven into the very fabric of my existence.

Acknowledgement

To the one who has touched my soul in ways words can scarcely express - your impact has been the light that guides me, the strength that lifts me, and the warmth that comforts me through every moment. With every beat of my heart, I am reminded of the profound imprint you have left on my life. You have transformed the extraordinary into something timeless, and for that, I am endlessly grateful.

This collection is a reflection of your influence on me - a force that has reshaped my world beyond imagination. Thank you, with all my heart, for everything.

Preface

You are the inspiration behind every word, every line, and every rhyme. Thank you for being the heartbeat of this collection. You have breathed life into these poems, and it is to you, with all my heart, that I offer this book.

May every word in the book resonate with you, as they were not merely written with ink, but woven from the deepest parts of my soul.

YOU MEAN EVERYTHING

You are the force that keeps him still,
You are his heartbeat, his very will.
You are the hymn
that wakes the dawn in him,
You are the reason his sky blooms with color,
Without you, gone is the valour

Your laughter builds the walls of his heart,
Your absence makes it go haywire.
Without you,
Gone is the warmth, gone is the fire.
You are the only language
His soul has learned to speak.
In your absence, his future feels bleak.

Without you, he is a prisoner of silence,
His sun will dim forever.
He will be left in pieces
The day he feels you untying yourself

From the threads you have woven together.

Each spot, each mark, each dent,
A story of laughter or love.
And you are the color in his gray.
Every morning, your light is the reason
He wakes with purpose.
What's life without you?
Nothing but a hollow.
You are the lighthouse
He is born to follow.

You're the reason he still believes
In the beauty of this world.
Remember the summers
When the sun melted into the sea,
And you swore the horizon
Belonged to only you two?
The world will turn colorless
When there's no YOU.

You're the first thought
When the sun wakes him.
You're the only thing
That makes the dark bearable.
Without you, the sky would lose its stars,
And the earth would forget how to spin.
Without you,
He is an entity miserable.

It's not just love—

You're his one constant,
The only thing that feels real
In a world that keeps shifting.
In your absence,
His spirit would be rifting.

You aren't just a part of his life;
You are his life.
You are the map of his heart,
Each moment with you a landmark.
Without you,
He is just a paper so blank.

If you were to leave,
He would lose himself entirely.
You are the compass
That keeps him from falling apart
You mean more to him

Than you could ever understand.
You are his hope,
You are his light,
You are his days so bright,
You are his night.

He doesn't know the words to say,
How much you mean in every way.
Each glance, a chapter, each touch, a line,
You are his only story in love's design.

No one could pen what you mean,
A love eternal, pure, unseen.
For to him, the world is slim—
It begins and ends with you, his dream.

Your laughter, the music he keeps,
Your tears, the ocean where he weeps.
In your absence, time stands still,
Even his soul bends to your will.

You mean to him what light means to day,
You are his guiding force, a constant stay.
Without you, the world feels dim,
Without you, gone is all charm.
You carry all of his dreams,

Like rivers cradling moonlit streams.
Each word you speak, a precious stone,
Inside his heart, you've built a home.

He watches you with tender care,
His entire universe began right there.
In your smile, the sun takes flight,
You are his dawn, you are his night.

You are his destination,
You are his path
No distance can ever
Erase this truth.
You're the thread that holds him whole,
You're the anchor tethered to his soul
Every step he takes, you're near.
All his life, he is yours, dear.

His moments are molded in the shape of you,
His days are painted with your hue.
The world could crumble,
The walls could fall,
But you are the reason he stands tall.

You're life's embrace, not just love,
A universe wrapped in a single wave.
Please never ever go, never stray,
For without you, the stars fade away.

You're the echo in his quiet mind,
Someone so passionate, you will never find.
You are his answer to a prayer unspoken,
A bond unyielding and never broken.

In his heart, you've drawn a crowd.
He might not always speak it loud.
Every beat repeats what words can't say,
That you are his night, his every day
The sky could fall, the stars could fade,
Only for your love, his soul was made.
You're his warmth in the coldest night,
You are reason he still finds the light.

Millions of voices could call his name,
But yours alone, sets his heart aflame.
The tender palm of yours, he holds with care,
A love so pure, beyond compare.
You are his morning, his midnight star,
You are the home he seeks,
No matter how far.

You are his summer sun,
You are his midnight moon,
You are the gentle breeze,
You are the autumn trees.
Each glance of yours, each word you say,
Colors his life in every way.

When the world turns cold, you are his fire,
You are the dream that lifts him higher.
You're the ground beneath his feet,
You are the rhythm in his heartbeat.
Without you, his world grows dim,
You are simply everything to him.

In his heart, your name is sung,
Timeless sagas forever young.
You are every hope, every dream, every whim,
You simply mean everything to him.
You are his lighthouse,
Unyielding and bright,

The one he believes will guide him through night.

You are the morning dew,
Fresh and pure,
You are his constant truth,
Take it for sure.

You are the whisper in the winds that pass,
You are the love eternal
Built to last.
Without you, he loses his way,
Dark is the night and sunless is the day.
For in his life, through thick and slim,
You are simply everything to him.

You are the walls that secure his soul,
You are the only one, who makes him whole.
No storm could shake, no darkness could
steal.
The love for you,
That he does deeply feel

You are his ocean, vast and deep,
The place where peacefully
All his dreams sleep.
Each wave a moment, fierce and strong,
Yours is the love he carries all along.
For his universe, though vast and grim,
It's all bright because you mean all to him.
To him, you're more than the earth or sea,
Beyond all ages, beyond infinity.
You mean more than the world could skim,
You are simply everything to him.

PLEASE DON'T GO AWAY

The first of hug of yours,
He shivered within,
The chill it created
Ran down his spine.
He will cherish it
For all of his years.
But without you around,
He drowns in tears.

Morning, evening,
Or even the night,
Without you,
Everything will fall,
Just short of slight.
That "slightest" even if it is
Means the world,
And means heart beats,
And means the breath,

And means happiness,
In the life of his......

Maybe,
One-day, he will be gone,
Beyond your any stretch of imagination.

The clouds would gather,
And so would the stars.
The wounds will heal,
But left will be the scars.

Deep in the ocean,
The tears get lost
We quite wonder -
Did I move on –
When I only needed to bide?

The dew drops of winter,
Would be still dancing on the tip of the leaf.
Will be it be a moment to cherish,
Or just a mournful eve?

Farther from forest we move,
Too close to the tree.
Is that what we call
The price of being free?

Dreams mean a lot

So do our aspirations.
All only in a moment's rapture,
Do they hold meaning
When we lose the
Shoulder to cry on?
Life sometimes
Is a chapter complicated,
Impossible to hold together
The pieces so shattered.

We fall, we rise,
We cry, we smile,
We still yearn for a soul to share
The feelings we pile

One gentle hug,

One tender kiss—
And when it's gone,
How much we miss.

Someone, somewhere,

Cares for you.

Without them,
If they fade from view,
We really wonder—
Where did we blunder?

We come, we go,
The river still flows.
Hang on to the moment
Before it goes.

If rose has a thorn,
Then the thorn has a rose.
Incomplete is the life
When only one we choose.

Years to build up,

And a moment to break—
Should true trust
Be such a fragile creak?

He is all for you,

And you are his princess.

You are his pulse,
The breath in his chest.
You are his damsel,
He lives in distress.
Some are overt
Some outspoken
But he is the one
Who fails to express.
What if next morning,
He is all gone?
What if next morning,
Exists there none?
Nothing is left but a
Giant black hole
What if next morning
Gone is the soul?

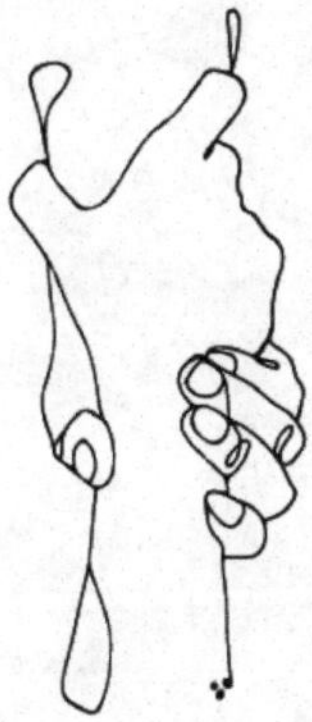

Hold on a little,

Dear,

Hold on a little.
Life is big, but
You need to trust a little.
Gather the pieces,
Put them amass
Together, you build
An unshakeable castle.
Never ever give up on him,
Never ever whittle.

Times change,
And so do our dreams.
The wind blows harder,
Directions change.

Hold on to the palm,
That's tender and calm.
Hold on to the hands,
Hold on with might.
End of the tunnel,
And there comes the light.

Easy to give up
When going gets tough
Easy to give in
When patch is rough.

Don't go away, dear,
Don't go away.
In difficult times,
People and opinions flood.
Hold on to the one you know,
Don't be under sway.

You are his dream,
You are his star.
You the bright spot
In his life a somber.
Today is the day
When you are upset,

Hang still upon him
Never ever give up.

One pinprick to you,
And bleeds his heart.
One drop of tear from
Your beautiful eyes
Drowns his heart
In the ocean of tears.
Sometimes he speaks,
Sometimes he may not.
Don't ever break up, dear,
Don't you ever go.
Morning will be there again,
And the sun will glow.

Woods are dark,

Sky is dark,

Roads are dark,
Times are dark,
Today is the day,
Lost is every spark.
Do not lose him further
At this time of need
Brightens up your world
With you being together.

You are his life,
His universe you are.
Alive he is, but
His heart beat you are.

When you are not around,
Toxic is the air,
In your absence, dear,

Gone is all valour.

He makes you smile,
He makes you whine,
He makes you burst into laughter.
For him, his whole life,
Only you are sought after.

One small tide, and
Sweeps away the sand.
Hold onto his hand,
Together you both,
Rooted is the stand.

Days are long,
Nights stretch wide,
Sometimes he even
Misses your fights.
Words you say,
You say no more.
Silence of yours,
Tears his core.

Life is short,
Dreams are many,
Without you,
He is not worth,

Even a penny.
Hold on to him,
He is for sure,
Always for you,
Not a fake lure.

Time is rough

You are sad,
It's but natural
That pain seeps through.
But retain your trust,
Don't lose the thrust.

Your self-belief
Will give you relief.
No one can judge,
There is no fudge,
Be with him,
Please don't budge.

We work hard,
But destiny decides.
Whatever comes our way,

Hope still presides.
Nothing is lost
When you are together.
Both of you can
Shake all heavens
And move every star.

You are the best,
Always for him.
He will go all out
To make you cherish.
Whatever you dream,
Hold his hands, dear,
Don't you depart.
Never ever will
Go in vain
Any of the effort.

Today is a time when
Things look doomed,
As if an endless
Tragedy has loomed.
Remember, though,
There is always a way.
All grief, with time,
Finally go away.
We cry, we creep,
We weep, we are sad.
One fine morning,
We see
All tears fade away.

Rises the sun
In the sky of our life,
Brightens our day
Once again.

Gone is the strife.
Hold on to your breath dear,
Hold onto his hand,
Together in problems,
Unshaken you stand.

One tender kiss
And one gentle hug,
Few moments with him
And you will feel smug.
Into his arms,
And into his heart,
Give in to your grievance
And forget the rest.

You are the number one,
But he is your zero.
You to his right,
And he becomes a hero.
But he becomes zero again,
When you are gone.

No valor, no pride—
There exists none.
Part away has no value,
Together you are ten on ten.
Never ever give up on him,
You are his gem.

Remember the blue beach,
Remember the rocks.
He holds you tight
When comes the tide.
Orange is the sun
On the west horizon,
Evening would fade away,
Slowly into night.
Together you become
A heavenly sculpture,
Into each other in love
Relish the rapture.

Remember the evenings
You cooked him dinner,
Filled with your love it was
He used to savour.

You put your heart
In the dish delicious.
Kiss on your lips—
He is lost in joy.
Do not ever go away, dear,
He is your boy.

Silent as you are today,
He is half dead
Speak from your heart,
Scold or sought
Please save his breath
Before he is nought.

Remember the days
He took you for a ride so long
Remember the songs
When he sang his heart out
Roads are empty
The stretch is long
You are so cozy
In his arms so strong

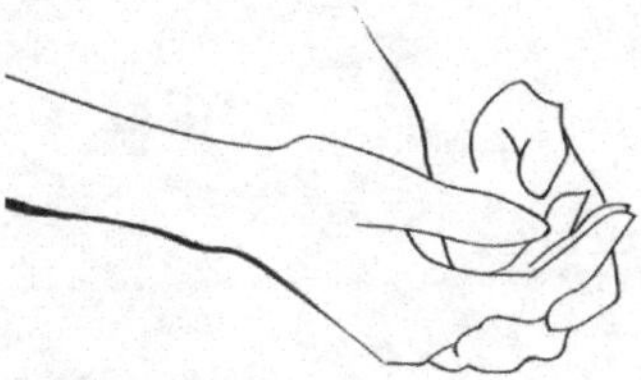

Starry is the night,
Moon so bright,
Hearts in love,
Beating so fast.
Two innocents,
Swains in the
World so vast.
Mistakes are human,
He too is the same.
Forgive him, please,
He takes all the blame.

Perfect is the enemy
Of the good, they say.
Universe of flaws, we live in,
Perfect is but nay.
We still get up,
We still try,
That is the only way

To someday touch the sky.
You are perfect still
In your own light.
Never ever give up, dear,
Never ever sway.

People will come,
People will go,
But some come to stay.
Spot out the rare ones,
They make your day.

He belongs to you,
In him, you believe.
Come what may,
Hold on to him,
He will never leave.

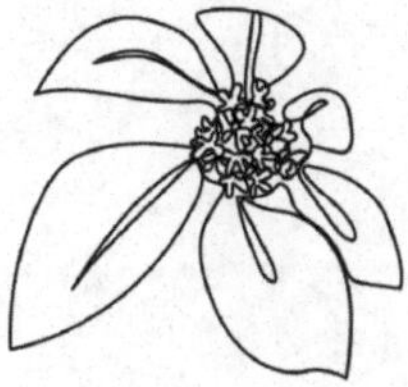

Silence of yours
Kills him each day,
But for your words,
Mad he become may.
Your sweet voice—
He longs for each moment,
Without your voice,
Nothing left to lament.

Remember the snow,
Remember the mountains,
Remember the winding roads,
Remember the silver fountains,
Remember the nights,
Remember the lights ,
Everything felt full of life.
With you by his side,
Life is never worth any strife.
Always remember,

In his life,
You are the one and only.
Without you,
In the middle of a crowd,
He still is lonely.

He says-
When it's morning, I long for you.
When it's evening, I ache for you.
When it's twilight, I yearn for you.
I miss you in the clouds,
I miss you in the rain,
I miss you in the stars,
I miss you in the moon.
When you are apart,
I miss you every moment.

When you are apart,
It's pure torment.
When you are far off,
Every terrain is a desert.
When you are far off,
It's a torture every moment.
When you are far off,
Every little while do I lament.
You are the only oasis
In this boundless desert.
You are the only hope,
Without you,
There's nothing but a deject.
It's tough for you,
He knows it well,
What all he feels,
He can't even tell.
Your journey is rough,
He knows it well,

He wishes you the best on the earth,
He knows you will be tough.
You are the best,
You are the sweetest,
You stand out in the crowd,
You are the star the brightest.

He is there for you,
No matter how far he is.
His heart beats for you,
No matter how far he is.
If you are upset,
His world goes upside down.
Without you,
He's just a clown.

He is just a tiny speck
In the vast canvas of sadness.
He is a just nothing,
In the hoards of mongers.
He is a shadow
Without a figure.
He is so small,
Without a measure.
You add everything to him,

You are his existence.
You bring colours to his life,
You bring him the brilliance.
You stand by him,
He stands tall.
Without you,
He is nothing at all.

He cares for every little thing about you,
He struggles to often express it to you.
He cares for your well-being,
He wishes you every good thing.
Sometimes, he seems a little awkward,
But he is always
Your orderly steward.
He loves you from the core of his heart,
He cares for you every tiny bit.

He breathes for you,
He lives for you,
He walks for you,
He stops for you,
He leans for you,
He stands for you,
He bends for you,
He mends for you.

With you does he smile,
With you does he cry,
With you only open he is,
And sometimes shy.
When you are upset,
Only emptiness prevails.
When you are hurt
His world shatters under pain.

Every memory is a treasure,
Keep it in custody,
Together, you cherish it,
Together, you relive,
Together, you laugh,
And burst into the rapture.
Small understandings
And little forgiveness
Will make both able to sustain
And retain,
Those tight hugs,
And those gentle kisses.

When you are upset,
His days turn black.
Sun becomes just a fiery red circle,

Slides down into the mountains,
Leaves his every hope in dark.
When you are silent,
Your silence kills,
Within just a moment
Life loses its thrills.

When you speak nothing,
He dwells into sorrow,
He falls into a vacuum,
His thoughts get fractured,
And his dreams lose the string.

Together, you sparkle,
Together, you glitter,
Together, you make the world
Beautiful and better.
You are the best,
And you are his universe,
Without you by his side,
He is a loser.
Life is tough, and so are the days,
Please don't lose faith in him,
Please don't desert him.

Without you there, beside him,
His days are sad,
And his nights are grim.

Trust, trust, and trust—
For anything to succeed,
It counts the most,
He is yours and only yours.
Never ever distrust dear
The love that he pours.
Life is a journey,
Destiny unknown,
So as the destination.
Let all egos melt down,
And let all hearsay go away.
May love win,
And may win you and your
This true companion.

Journey is difficult,
Full of thorns,
Focus on the flower,
Focus on the rose.
You will flourish,
You will shine the most.

Hold on to him forever,
Never ever lose him,
Never let him lose.

When you are silent,
His days are gloomy,
His nights are doomy,
His dreams are gone,
He has hopes none.
He is so sad,
His time is bad.
Talk to him a word,
Before he goes mad.

Rainbow holds colours in seven,
He carries colours by the million.
All are for you and all are by you
Without you, he is colourless,
His persona is just lustreless.
You make him fly,
You make him soar high.
Without you,
He loses his wings,
He falls down down in the air,
On the earth rough and dry.
Without you,
His sky loses colours, and
Shine alludes the stars,
Gone is the smile,
Left is all vile, and
All his dreams become
Deadly nightmares.

All the words he speaks,
He feels for you.
He may look shallow,
But his feelings are real.
And deep inside,
He's truly hollow.

He is with you,
In good and in bad.
He is with you,
In smiles and tears.
He is with you,
When you are happy,
And when you are sad.
He will be there,
For you forever.
He will be there,
For you in every sphere.
Your interest is
His greatest concern.
Your happiness is
His only wish.
You rise to your best,
He cares for you.
You excel beyond the rest,

He aspires for you.

You are his glory,
You are his pride.
He cares only for you,
Always by your side.
He wants you to shine,
He wishes you joy.
He wishes you success,
He is your boy.

He has got nothing to hide.
You there with him,
The journey of life
Is just a pleasant a ride.

Days are bright,
Darkness becomes light.
Shine the stars,
Dreams take flight.
Without you,
He is fully lost.
When you are away,
He is a living ghost.
His eyes are wet,

His heart is broken,
In the silhouette of daylight,
Upon him falls sunset,
Never ever go away.
Never ever leave him.
He loves you deep inside.
But for you,
He can't leave anymore.
He will be left petrified.
His commitment to you,
Is beyond all questions.
His dedication to you,
Is beyond any doubt.
Nothing he won't do for you,
His love is beyond count.

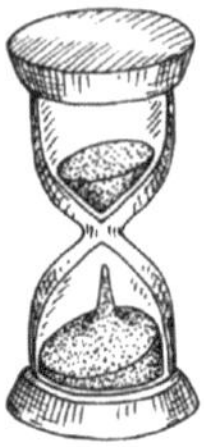

Time flies,

And with time,
His love only grows.
His feelings for you
Never ever slows.
When he is asleep,
He dreams of you,
When he is awake.
It's always you in his thought.
Without you, even for a moment,
Life becomes so fraught.
Fragile are hopes sometimes,
Volatile are relations.
Here is a man,
Stands rock solid.
Respects your emotions,
Cares for your well-being.
His heart is pure,
And not even a bit squalid.

Dew drops on the leaves
Make mornings so beautiful,
But when you don't talk to him,
Life is so lull,
And sun looks so dull,
Morning starts as an aimless toddler,
Day passes off wayward,
Evening is cladded with melancholy,
Night is only dark and quavered.

In his heart,
The daffodils dance,
The sunflowers blossom,
The marigolds make merry,
And the chrysanthemums become
cacophonous,
The orchard turns into orchestra,
When your lips are leery,
Autumn sets in,
In the middle of spring,
All the flowers shrivel,
All the leaves wither,
And all the greenery fade,
Even for a moment baby,
If your eyes are ever teary.

In the realm of divine love,
We only ascend,
It gets more and more pure everyday,
When we care,
We nurture it like a plant,
Sometimes the flowers wither,
Sometimes the leaves fall down,
But remember dear,
This is only a phase,
And even this shall pass away,
Just hold onto each other with trust,
And stand by each other like a pillar,
Sooner than later,
You are the winner.

Keep it simple
Keep it light
In his arms
Hold him tight
Time passes off
So should be the fight
In true love
Everything is right
He is your man
He is your choice
Without you
He has no voice
Let the spark glow
Till eternity
Do stay with each other
Till infinity.

Love makes the world go round
Love takes life beyond any bound

Love needs understanding
Love needs love
Love is innocent
Love is pure
Sometimes an infant
Sometimes mature
Love is simply incomprehensible
Visible at times
Some day invisible.

Love never has any definition
Love cannot be given a connotation
We fall in love to rise otherwise
Every omen goes off
When love strikes.

He is your lucky champ
You are his Lady
You are his need and
He is the needy
Life is a journey
Humps and plains
With he by your sides
The pain subsides
Life is a series of endless dreams

In all darkness
He will always be
The true light beams.

Let your heart, gently pout out
Don't hold it tight
If your heart pounds
Look for no bounds
Let it beat and beat for him
The way his heart beats for you
Let the breathings be in rhythm
Let there be written
A chapter all new - Where hearts entwine
Through every line
Through every rhyme
His love my dear
Is always true
He is a story
Written for you
With every page
A chapter grows
In silent whispers
Love bestows.